HOW TO THINK CREATIVELY AND PROSPER FINANCIALLY

HOW TO THINK CREATIVELY AND PROSPER FINANCIALLY

Steps To Living A Creative and Financially Prosperous Life

JEROHAM C. IBEH

Gushing Stream Publications Ltd Lagos - Nigeria

Contents

INTRODUCTION

Introduction

Prosperity, or to be prosperous, is the natural desire of all human beings. Every human being on planet earth desires to be thriving prosperously. Why? Because life itself is meant to be prosperous.

God never intended for anyone to fail. Failure is simply one's ignorance or disobedience to the laws that govern prosperity. To become prosperous, one must understand both the spiritual and physical laws of prosperity and align oneself with it.

There are only two kinds of people in the world: successful people and unsuccessful people. The difference between these two is that the successful ones are those who, by intense study, exploration, discipline, diligence, and obedience of faith, have discovered and mastered the laws that govern prosperity and have committed themselves to these laws, through which they have become prosperous and even super-prosperous.

On the other hand, the unsuccessful ones are those who do not think with their minds, who prefer to die than to think. They are those who believe in the illusion of something for nothing. They are those who sit around waiting for things to happen. They are those who are not in any way inclined towards studying, exploring, discipline, diligence, the obedience of faith, and the application of that which is learned. As the saying goes, *they are those who will not learn, unlearn, and relearn.* These are the failures, the unprosperous, and the unsuccessful ones in any nation of the world.

There are people who were not privileged to be a graduate of prominent and renowned universities, but today they own multi-billion and multimillion-dollar companies and are very successful in their various nations around the world because they went in search of the laws that govern prosperity and they found it, understood it, and began living by it, and today they are super-prosperous.

The Scripture says: "*Ask, and it shall be given you; seek, and ye shall find; knock, and it shall be opened unto you: For every one that asketh receiveth; and he that seeketh findeth; and to him that knocketh it shall be opened.*" (Matthew 7:7-8).

That means until you ask, you don't receive anything. Until you seek, you are not permitted to find anything, and until you knock, the door remains shut at you.

However, the fact that you are holding this book in your hands right now is an indication that you are tired of maintaining the status quo, which is poverty in disguise, and now you desire to break out of the crowd and become uniquely outstanding.

The Chapters that follow contain the methods of how you can become highly productive and prosperous like never before, that if applied, will set you on the way of becoming that productive, successful, and financially prosperous person you have long desired.

Chapter I

CREATED TO CREATE

* * *

· *Created To Create*

My mission in this book is to stir up the creativity in you. That creative power that God had deposited inside of you before you became flesh and blood and was born into this world.

Whether you know or not, we all are born with creative powers. We all came into this world with seeds of creative abilities in our unique and different ways. The purpose of these seeds of creative powers is to impact lives, live prosperously and make a difference in the world for God's glory.

Our ability to create is vast and limitless because we are made and fashioned in the image and likeness of Him that is exceedingly vast, limitless, and unfathomable.

We are sons and daughters of light, and in His Light, we see the light that revealed to us our true identity, *beings endowed with the greatest seeds of creative powers.* Therefore, manifesting your divinity is what follows after you have discovered your divine identity.

An eagle that grows among chickens will always see himself as a chicken until the day he discovers his true identity. Only then will he begin to live as he should, *soaring in the sky and perching on the highest mountains.*

Great men and women, both past and present, become significant, not only by the discovery of their divine identity, they diligently mastered the art of stirring up their creative powers, and by so doing, continuously and consistently, they changed the world and amassed unlimited fortunes.

The most extraordinary seeds of creative powers have been made dormant in many lives due to the lack of self-knowledge. Miss-education and false understanding of self across the so-called developing nations are the reasons for all kinds of dysfunctions among those nations' institutions, political, economical, and otherwise.

Woe unto you, lawyers! **for ye have taken away the key of knowledge:** *ye entered not in yourselves, and them that were entering in, ye hindered. (Luke 11:52.).*

Conspiracy is the word. The revelation of self-identification is the key that opens the door to creative manifestations. God, by His Spirit, is revealing to us what men thought they have hidden from us. *"Surely in vain the net is spread in the sight of any bird."* (Proverbs 1:17.).

That is why I'm excited that you are reading this book because I'm going to share the fundamental principles you can continuously and consistently engage in to awaken the creative power lying dormant inside of you.

A wise man once said: *"The greatest misery that has befallen man is that man looks outside of himself to seek for the solution to his problems."*

The solution to your problems is right inside of you. So you don't have to look outside of yourself for solutions to your problems.

All you need is to master the art of stirring up your creative powers diligently, and you will have not only your problems solved, but you will also become a solution to the problems of others and the world at large.

You were created to create. Creativity is part of your making, and you cannot but manifest that which you are, once the principles for that manifestation are applied and abide. Financial prosperity is what happens when you begin to manifest your divinity, which is creativity.

Anytime you take out money from your wallet and pay for any item, you have just made the inventor or the producer of that item richer. That is why you must not look outside of yourself for solutions because you are the solution.

You came to this world as the solution for humanity's problem in one way or another. That is what Jesus Christ meant when he declared: "*Ye are the light of the world*". (Matthew 5:14).

If you leave this earth without fulfilling that purpose for which you were born, then you have disappointed God and failed humanity.

All the inventions that are aiding life and adding value to humanity in diverse ways today were made possible by men and women who manifested their divinity by stirring up that seed of creative power that God has deposited in each and every one of us and by manifesting their divinity they have acquired and continue to acquire wealth in abundance.

· *Thinking*

The key to genuine financial prosperity in life is creativity. Therefore, the first fundamental principle you must engage in stirring up your creative power is *thinking*.

You must become a thinker, a creative thinker, a strategic thinker, and an inventive thinker. In other words, you must think creatively, strategically, and inventively.

When you look at products and services, do you see them just the way they are or how they should be? Do you see the world the way it is or the way it should be? As you go out and come in on a daily basis, what do you see as the people's needs? And in what way or ways do you think that need can be met?

Your answer, or answers to these questions determine whether you are thinking creatively or not. Or do you ignore the people's complaints about what they need and expect the government to meet that need? Or have you dismissed the fact that what we call government is just a group of individuals like you and I who temporarily occupy executive offices who also need the collective efforts of its citizens to function?

With their elaborate office surroundings and numerous secretaries and clerks, they put on a show that causes people to hold them in awe. Just bear in mind that these executives we call governments are mere human beings with the same fears, the same frailties, limitations, and faults that are common to everyone. They are nothing but pliant souls at their homes, and they understand that they cannot govern and prosper their nations without their fellow citizens' creative abilities.

Every good government empowers its citizens from every angle with quality education for the development of the minds of its citizens, and it's open to the creative ideas from its citizens except where there is a conspiracy within that government.

Conspiracy is inevitable in many corrupt nations around the world where leaders fraudulently embezzle and misappropriate public funds that are supposed to be used in educating and developing the minds of their people, and by that continuous practice of misappropriation of public funds, many so-called leaders have left their nations worthless and poor even with the gold, oil, diamond, and other mineral resources beneath their soil, because it takes creative minds to utilize resources for the greater good of all. Leadership, therefore, is accountability born out of responsibility; otherwise, it a fraudulent activity.

In nations where the leaders always congregate to discuss more and more on how to constantly and continuously invest in educating and developing the minds of their people practically in every field of human endeavor, leadership is made easy in those nations, and the standard of living for the citizens of such nations continue to improve in every way.

Therefore, as an agent of change, you must find out what the people need and then think on the possibilities through which that need or needs can be met. That is why you are on this earth, to solve problems via that seed of creative power that God has placed inside of you.

The people's complaints are your opportunity to make money and become rich. If you ignore the people's complaints, you deny yourself the golden opportunity of achieving financial prosperity.

According to Dr. *Robert E. Franken, "thinking creatively means the tendency to generate or recognize ideas, alternatives, or possibilities that may be useful in solving problems ."*

That means you must brainstorm to generate or recognize ideas, alternatives, and possibilities that can be converted to solve a problem or problems.

To think creatively, you must learn and understand that time comes when you just have your own unique ways of doing things without violating anyone's right. Doing things in your

own unique way or ways is one of the fundamental art of creativity and inventiveness.

As the educator and business consultant
Shiv Khera said: *"Winners don't do different
things. They do things differently"*.

To think creatively, you must break out of
the influences and patterns of society. In this
world, the majority is not using their minds.
They are always looking out of themselves to
someone or something somewhere for a solution.

That is why a wise man once said: *that out
of the 100 percent of the world's population,
only 5 percent think, 15 percent think that they
are thinking, and the remaining 80 percent
rather die than to think.*

Break out of the crowd and be outstanding.
You cannot be following the crowd and expect
to think creative thoughts because the majority
is not thinking at all.

The Scripture says: "*And be not conformed to this world: but be ye transformed by the renewing of your mind, that ye may prove what is that good, and acceptable, and perfect, will of God.*" (Romans 12:2).

You cannot walk in God's perfect will for your life if you are conformed to the ways of the world with its superficial values and customs, which has deceived and blinded the minds of many.

To think creative thoughts means to have fresh perceptions and insightful judgments. You must believe in yourself by believing what the word of God says about you.

Again, you were created to create. The seed of limitless creative powers resides inside of you. And God has provided you with the word of His Power on how to stir up and activate that creative power that He has deposited inside of you so that you can live a super-prosperous life and fulfill your purpose here on the earth.

You may not have to create something new. By adding value to something that exists already and making it better and more accessible for people to use can make you rich overnight.

All you have to do is come up with creative ideas, and there are companies out there who have the money to buy that idea or ideas from you and make it their own or sponsor the idea or ideas and share the incomes with you, and before you know it you have become rich.

The problem with lots of people is not their country, the family they come from, not even their educational background. Because most of the great men and women we celebrate today in terms of creativity and financial prosperity did not even finish school. Some of them came from a very low-income family background. The problem with lots of people is their inability to *think creative thoughts.* They have time for everything but the time to think and brainstorm creatively.

I read this story some years back about Bill

Gates, the founder of Microsoft Inc, which I find interesting and imperative to reference here. The story revealed that Mr. Gates, when he was a teenager, has a habit of locking himself in his room to engage in creative thinking.

So one day, he was in his room thinking as usual, and his mom, unaware of his whereabouts, began calling out to him, "Bill, where are you?" Young Bill then couldn't hear his mom calling because he was deep in thoughts. So the mom came to his room to see if he is there, and to her surprise, there was Bill, lost in thoughts, and she said to him, "Bill, didn't you hear me call?" Young Bill, looking at his mom, who has just interrupted his creative thinking activity, said to the mom: *"can't you see I'm thinking, don't you think?"*

Today, Mr. Bill Gates is one of the world's wealthiest people with a net worth $115 Billion as I write this book. He is financially prosperous because he mastered the art of investing his time in *thinking creative thoughts* through which he could generate or recognize ideas, alternatives, or possibilities that is now useful in solving multiple global problems today.

· *Invest Time*

Everyone on earth, whether rich or poor, young or old, black or white, all have the same twenty-four hours a day. Whether you are living in Africa, America, Europe, Asia, or down in Australia, wherever you are located, you have the same measure of time everyone has every day, *twenty-four hours.*

Now, what you do with the twenty-four hours you are given every day is what makes the difference, and it's also what differentiates you from others.

You must have heard the saying that time is the currency of life, which stands to reason that, if you waste time, you waste life. Time, therefore, is everything.

Successful people invest their time in creative thinking, generating, and putting together ideas to solve a human problem by which they acquire wealth. In contrast, unsuccessful people spend or squander their time on futility, which clutters the mind and makes the individual ineffective. No wonder they are unsuccessful.

To think creatively, strategically, and inventively, you must always appreciate time and invest it into creative thinking, because the more you engage in creative thinking, the more your ability to think creatively grows.

That is the winning secret of successful people; they always think and think until they start *thinking without thinking* because you can only become perfect at what you practice. The more you do anything, the easier it becomes.

Set out time to think. Practice self-isolation from family, friends, and love once, so that you can be alone to generate or recognize ideas through creative thinking.

In this world, everything is calling for your attention, so you must practice self-isolation so that you can be alone to think without any side attractions, which causes only distractions.

The TV in your sitting room is calling for your attention. Your spouse, children, family, and friends are all calling for your attention. Even the social media apps on your phone and the billboards on the roadsides are all calling for your attention. All of these things are side attractions, which causes only distractions when it comes to creative thinking. So you must deal with these side attractions through self-isolation so that you can be alone to generate ideas through creative and innovative thinking.

Great inventors who have added value to humanity through their inventions were known for spending hours every day in their laboratories, thinking and experimenting to ensure that they arrive at the desired results, and they did.

Thomas A. Edison was always found experimenting in his laboratory. He experimented ten thousand times to arrive at his desired result at a time, and he was quoted saying: *"I have not failed. I've just found 10,000 ways that won't work."*

While it's essential that you practice self-isolation to engage in creative and innovative thinking, it's also vital that you practice that isolation with an empty stomach.

You can call it fasting if you will, but it's crucial that you practice creative thinking on an empty stomach because it makes you feel sharper by enhancing the cognitive processes of gaining knowledge and comprehension, which also includes thinking, knowing, remembering, judging, and problem-solving, which is the purpose for creative thinking; to solve problems. Fresh fruits and mineral water is perfect during your creative thinking exercise.

Always eat less and exercise more. Too much food in the stomach dulls the mind and weakens its ability to think creatively and inventively. So ensure that your mind is always alert and sharp so that you can think and produce astonishing ideas.

· *Thinking Materials*

To engage in creative thinking, you must gather the right materials and take them with you as you go on self-isolation for creative thinking exercise. Gathering the right materials for your creative thinking exercise is very important so that you will not waste your time.

As a Christian, the Bible is your number one material when engaging in creative, strategic, and inventive thinking. But unfortunately, religiosity has made many minds to lack its elasticity and versatility, without which the mind is limited to think analytically to solve problems. That is because the Bible is seen by many as a religious text when in actuality, it's not. The Bible is a Book of wisdom and spiritual counsels through which one can prosper and live a life that is approved of God.

Read the following verse carefully and see for yourself how Paul the apostle, when writing to Timothy, defined the Bible:

"All Scripture is inspired by God and is useful for teaching the truth, rebuking error, correcting faults, and giving instruction for right living." (2 Timothy 3:16. GNT).

That means when you commit yourself to the study of the Bible; you are inspiring your mind with the Inspiration of God because *all Scripture is inspired by God.*

The Bible furnishes your mind with truth. It reprimands you of errors, teaches you how to correct faults, and counsels you with instructions on how to live a super-prosperous and fulfilled life. What else do you need!

If you read the 17th verse of that same chapter, it says that the study and practice of

Scriptures *make you complete, and proficient, outfitted, and thoroughly equipped for every good work.* The Bible, therefore, is an essential Book you cannot do without if you must achieve something astonishing in your creative thinking exercise.

The King James Version and the Amplified Version of the Bible are perfect for your creative thinking routing. You can get other versions, but the King James Version and the Amplified Version of the Bible are perfect for a start.

History has records of great inventors who immersed themselves deeply into the study of Scriptures and were inspired by God's Inspiration to arrive at their desired inventions through which many problems in the world are solved today.

Some of these inventors were Michael Faraday (1791 – 1867), James Clerk Maxwell (1831 – 1879), and many others, to name a few.

The Bible is your guide in the affairs of life. It points to you the right way to go and instructs you on the best decisions to make. "*Thy word is a lamp unto my feet, and a light unto my path.*" (Psalm 119:105).

The Bible is a wonderful counselor that has never failed when believed and applied in faith. The knowledge of the Scriptures makes you wise. It catapults you into unusual insights and protects you from deceptions and manipulations.

Knowledge of the Scriptures are the winning secrets of life: "*Thou through thy commandments hast made me wiser than mine enemies: for they are ever with me. I have more understanding than all my teachers: for thy testimonies are my meditation. I understand more than the ancients, because I keep thy precepts*". (Psalm 119:98-100).

Do not ignore the Bible in your quest for creative, strategic, and inventive thinking.

"Seek ye out of the book of the Lord, and read: no one of these shall fail, none shall want her mate: for my mouth, it hath commanded, and his spirit it hath gathered them." (Isaiah 34:16.)

The word of God cannot fail because it does not have the ability to fail. So by carrying your Bibles with you in your creative thinking exercise, you are sure to encounter an idea or ideas that will bless your life and the world at large.

Chapter II

THE POWER OF BOOKS

* * *

· *The Power of Books*

....I Daniel understood by books....
(Daniel 9:2).

Books? Yes, books. Every great discovery begins with or is traceable to a book. Therefore, as you practice self-isolation to engage in creative thinking exercises, you must carry along with you great books that talk about the subject you are thinking on. This is very important!

Books sharpen your mind and increase your curiosity by which you gain depth of knowledge and understanding of yourself and your environment. Engaging in creative thinking exercise without a book or books is time and energy wasted in an exercise of futility.

"A room without books is like a body without a soul," says Marcus Tullius Cicero.

Gather books and gather not a few is a command, not a suggestion, because the Scripture teaches us to be filled with the knowledge of God's will **in all wisdom and spiritual understanding**. (See Colossians 1:9.).

Knowledge empowers your mind to think. So you must gather anointed books of greater minds in the kingdom to boost your depth of Scriptural knowledge and understanding, which aides your creative thinking exercise for astonishing ideas.

Again gather books and gather not a few. Fill up the spaces in your home with books. Light up your life with knowledge through books.

Spend money on books and eat them like food, and the knowledge gained will turn you into a manufacturer of goods and services that will solve human problems and, in turn, make you financially prosperous.

Through the habit of reading scientific books with the Scriptures, Michael Faraday became one of the most outstanding scientists in history.

After he was expelled from school because the teachers thought he could not learn, Thomas Edison immersed himself into reading books on inventions, and he became one of the greatest inventors in history.

History is filled with records of humble individuals from different backgrounds who solved lots of human problems and achieved greatness through the habit of explorative study of books and the application of that which they discovered.

Paul, the apostle, was a man of books, which is why he excelled in the gospel more than those who were with Christ from inception. In one of his letters to Timothy, he said:

*"When you come, bring the coat that I left at Troas with Carpus, and the **books**, especially the **parchments**." (2 Timothy 4:13 AMP).*

Paul, the apostle, couldn't stay without books and his notes (Parchments). No wonder he excelled significantly in the gospel message because he didn't allow God's grace upon his life to be in vain. (See 1 Corinthians 15:10). So he labored more abundantly than they all and received divine double honor because double honor is credited to those who labor in the word. (See 1 Timothy 5:17).

Don't walk pass through a bookstore without stopping by and grabbing some titles. Bookstores are the best places to always visit from time to time. Bookstores, whether online or otherwise, are places where you shop for answers to questions. Bookstores are places where you obtain answers that you cannot get via mouth to mouth. You understand!

In the parable of the Ten Virgins in Matthew 25, the wise virgins told the other ones that ran out of oil saying: .....*but go ye rather to them that sell and buy for yourselves.* (Verse 9). That is the best advice anyone can give -go *to them that sell and buy oil (books) for yourself.*

· *Listening To Classical Songs*

Utilize the power of classical songs as you self-isolate to engage in creative, strategic, and inventive thinking. Classical songs have a way of boosting your brain power by increasing your memory retention of what is learned.

Classical songs calm your nerves and make you concentrate on your thoughts undistracted. Research has proven that students who listen to classical songs when studying for exams scores more than those who do not. It has also been proven that loud or agitated music can have adverse effects on reading comprehension and mood, making focus more difficult.

Avoid loud music, both in your home and outside your home. Always maintain a tranquil environment so that you can always be alert to pick up the messages God is sending to your spirit, which are the creative ideas you seek.

Osagyefo Dr. Kwame Nkrumah, the first president and the founding father of The Republic of Ghana, was said to have, both at his office and in his bedroom, 155 Ghana high-life music and 265 classical songs, and he was not a fan of food.

That means Dr. Nkrumah was a man who utilized the power of classical songs. He also ate very less and focused more on creative thinking by which he was empowered to achieve independence for the then Gold Coast and led the country as Ghana under the Ghana Independence Act of 1957.

Also, in 2 Kings Chapter three, there was a situation, and the king Jehoshaphat needed to hear a word from a prophet of God, and he was told that Elisha was around, and they quickly went to Elisha. On getting there, they explained the situation to Elisha, expecting him to give them a word of prophecy on what should be done, but Elisha couldn't get a rhema. So he asked the king to get him a minstrel, and the Scripture declares:

.... *"And it came to pass, when the minstrel played, that the hand of the Lord came upon him. And he said, Thus saith the Lord, Make this valley full of ditches. For thus saith the Lord, Ye shall not see wind, neither shall ye see rain; yet that valley shall be filled with water, that ye may drink, both ye, and your cattle, and your beasts. And this is but a light thing in the sight of the Lord: he will deliver the Moabites also into your hand"*. (2 Kings 3:15-18.).

A minstrel is one who plays on a harp, and harp is one of the instruments that are used in classical songs. So we can say that Elisha demanded to hear a classical song, and as the song played, bam, rhema came, and he prophesied the answer needed to solve the problem.

Note this; classical songs do not give you rhema or ideas. It only positions you with the right attitude of mind to receive rhema or ideas by which problems are solved. Therefore, maintaining a serene environment and listening to classical songs are vital when studying and engaging in creative, strategic, and inventive thinking.

Moreover, the time you engage in your creative thinking exercise must be appropriate. You must have heard the saying that *"5:30 am is when great people are either going to bed or rising."* That means you must either be awake all night to pray, engage in study and creative thinking and then go to bed at 5:30 am. Or go to bed early to rise early at 5:30 am, study, think, pray and then begin your day. Those are the best hours to study and engage in creative thinking. It's the most fruitful time.

I enjoy the hours between 2:00 am to 6:00 am. That is why I go to bed early to be awake earlier to pray, study, think, write, and then start my day. Sometimes I stay up all night in my study till 5:30 am and begin my day straight up, and then during the day, I will take some nap to make up the night vigil.

So you must choose between those hours for your prayers, study and creative thinking exercise, and watch your life flourish like the palm tree and grow like a cedar in Lebanon. (See Psalm 92:12).

Finally, you must master the art of taking a nap during the day. In creative thinking exercise, you need energy and alertness of mind and body, and that is what you get after taken a nap.

"The replenishing thing that comes with a nap - you end up with two mornings in a day".
-Pete Hamill.

I don't miss a nap during the day because it reinforces me with energy and refreshes my mind for night study if I have to stay up at night.

When you take a nap, you wake up refreshed and invigorated, and then you can engage in

creative thinking with absolute focus and con-
centration without any feelings of tiredness.

Thirty to forty minutes nap is often the best, but it should not exceed one hour. The best time to take a nap during the day is between 1:30 pm and 2:30 pm. And make sure you have already eaten lunch, if you have to, and with less or zero fat, before taking a nap. Some of the feelings of dizziness during active duty are due to fatty foods in the stomach.

Leaving everything you are doing during the day for thirty to forty minutes to take a nap is a great thing, and you've got to master this art if you must think strategically, creatively, and inventively.

· *Creative Efforts*

The last but not the least, is creative effort. Creative effort is what enables you to bring your ideas into reality. You must understand that you will begin to receive ideas and revelations as you practice self-isolation to engage in creative thinking.

It may be an idea to create a new product or to modernize an existing one with better features for better use. It can also be an idea to solve a personal or global problem. Whatever the idea, it will require some personal but creative effort to bring that idea into reality.

Once you are able to generate or recognize an idea during your creative thinking exercise, take action immediately to bring that idea into reality. Don't procrastinate. Don't go around telling people about your sound idea. Take the necessary steps and bring that idea into reality. That is what creative efforts are all about.

The creative effort to bring your idea to reality requires courage, boldness, and fearlessness. You must be courageous and banish fear and timidity from your mind if you must bring your idea to the limelight.

The only thing that stands between you and the success you desire is *yourself.* So apply creative efforts. If your idea is to set up a children's library where children can come and read books and get inspired, then step out and start doing it without procrastination.

If your idea is to bring a new product into the market that will solve many problems and meet lots of needs, then start doing it and get it done.

If you don't have enough money to start at the time, then prepare your business proposal with a well-detailed plan, and take it to the bank for loan or sponsorship, and surely, in one way or the other, your idea or ideas will come to the limelight as long as your efforts remain creative.

Now, get to work with these keys of prosperity. Make them part of your life from today, and you will become one of the creative, significant, and financially prosperous people in the world. You were made to live in prosperity. Nothing can stop you, but *yourself*!

ABOUT THE AUTHOR

JEROHAM C. IBEH is the author of The Seven Principles, The Wisdom for Mighty Works, and Mastering the Forces of Success. He is also the founder and the head pastor of The Greater Success House of God, a Christian Church organization that focuses on the teachings of Biblical Applications for Prosperous and Successful Living. Having studied Christian Theology, Christian Leadership and Youth Ministry at the Christian Leaders Institute in Spring Lake, Michigan USA, Jeroham C. Ibeh has passionately dedicated his life to teaching and impacting lives globally with the teachings on Biblical Application for Successful Living, which he termed "The Knowledge of the Truth." He lives in Nigeria with his wife and children.

By Jeroham C. Ibeh

- The Wisdom For Might Works

- The Seven Principles

- Mastering The Forces Of Success

- The Knowledge of Wisdom

- How To Think Creatively And Prosper Financially

Gushing Stream Publications Ltd

Lagos - Nigeria

Email: gushingstreampublications@gmail.com

Follow us on Facebook and Instagram to stay up to date on your favorite books:-

facebook.com/GushingStream   instagram.com/GushingStream